193 00322 544

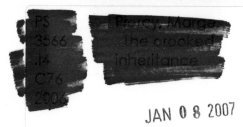

PS
3566
.I4
C76
2006

Percy, Marge
The crooked
inheritance

JAN 0 8 2007

D0952011

The Crooked Inheritance

THE
Crooked Inheritance

POEMS BY

MARGE PIERCY

ALFRED A. KNOPF · NEW YORK · 2006

THIS IS A BORZOI BOOK
PUBLISHED BY ALFRED A. KNOPF

Copyright © 2006 by Marge Piercy
All rights reserved under International and Pan-American Copyright
Conventions. Published in the United States by Alfred A. Knopf,
a division of Random House, Inc., New York, and simultaneously
in Canada by Random House of Canada Limited, Toronto.
Distributed by Random House, Inc., New York.
www.aaknopf.com

Knopf, Borzoi Books, and the colophon are
registered trademarks of Random House, Inc.

Library of Congress Cataloging-in-Publication Data
Piercy, Marge.
The crooked inheritance : poems / by Marge Piercy.—1st ed.
p. cm.
ISBN 0-307-26507-2
I. Title.
PS3566.I4C76 2006
813'.54—dc22   200604137

Manufactured in the United States of America
First Edition

CONTENTS

HOW TO MAKE PESTO

CHOOSE A COLOR

MATING

THE BIRTHDAY OF THE WORLD

TRACKS

A vision of horses and mules

Learn to think like a horse
her trainer said. She went
into the pasture at noon,
when her horses lay down to sleep
without fear of coyotes,
without fear. They sensed her
but did not mind as she stretched
out beside them with the June
heat's broad strong hand
flattening her into the grass.

Now, she said, I *am studying*
mules. Her trainer told her
horses forget everything by
and by. Mules never forget.
Carry your intention carefully,
a brimming bowl of water.
Mule skinner, I called her,
and from my childhood I saw
a tin of Boraxo my father used
to clean grease from his hands.

Twenty-mule teams crossed
the Death Valley of our bath
room, little black mules along
the bottom of the tin, the driver

in his wagon, the whip cracking
a wicked S in the air. I'm a mule:
stubborn, dragging heavy grudges,
joys and lost friends from the alkaline
mines of my past across the bleak
present to some future vital use.

Tracks

The small birds leave cuneiform
messages on the snow: I have
been here, I am hungry, I
must eat. Where I dropped
seeds they scrape down
to pine needles and frozen sand.

Sometimes when snow flickers
past the windows, muffles trees
and bushes, buries the path,
the jays come knocking with their beaks
on my bedroom window:
to them I am made of seeds.

To the cats I am mother and lover,
lap and toy, cook and cleaner.
To the coyotes I am chaser and shouter.
To the crows, watcher, protector.
To the possums, the foxes, the skunks,
a shadow passing, a moment's wind.

I was bad watchful mommy to one man.
To another I was forgiving sister
whose hand poured out honey and aloe;
to that woman I was a gale whose lashing

waves threatened her foundation; to this
one, an oak to her flowering vine.

I have worn the faces, the masks
of hieroglyphs, gods and demons,
bat-faced ghosts, sibyls and thieves,
lover, loser, red rose and ragweed,
these are the tracks I have left
on the white crust of time.

The crooked inheritance

A short neck like my mother
long legs like my father
my grandmother's cataract of hair
and my grandmother's cataracts
my father's glaucoma
my mother's stout heart
my father's quick temper
my mother's curiosity
my father's rationality
my mother's fulsome breasts
my father's narrow feet

Yet only my grandmother saw in me
a remembrance of children past
You have a good quick mind like Moishe.
Your grandfather zecher l'vrocho
had a gift for languages too.
Rivka also had weak eyes
and a delicate stomach.
You can run as fast as Feygeleh.
You know that means little bird?

I was a nest of fledglings chirping
hunger and a future of flight
to her, but to my parents,
the misshapen duckling

who failed to make flesh
their dreams of belonging:
a miraculous blond angel
who would do everything
right they had failed.
Instead they got a black
haired poet who ran away.

Seven horses

When I was a pencil of a girl
I had seven horses, one
for each day of the week.

Thunder, Lightning, Sun
and Moon, East Wind
North Wind and Red Roses.

Only I could see them,
roan and black, grey,
palomino, dapple, white

and the strange one,
the flying red horse
from the Mobil sign.

I rode them to school,
home, to the store.
I rode them down the slopes

of rocky night. In adolescence
I never mooned over horses.
Later, they were something cops

charged at us in demonstrations.
I'd sooner ride a cow.
No, it was not horseflesh

but power I craved
and speed. I longed to gallop
out of our tight mortgaged house

furnished with shouts and razors,
out of the smoke of frustrations
burning like old tires.

I wanted to stick out my neck
and gallop at full tilt off
any map I had ever seen.

Muttering

Muttering: the word in which
I find the mother, *die mutter.*
Women without power mumble
curses, feathery threats as
they dust, as they stir the soup.

The soup ends up too salty,
as if the broth were tears.
He—the italicized husband—
promised me and didn't.
I asked and he wouldn't.

How could he call me that?
She bangs the pot down
on the burner. Down into
the basement she drags
her prayers, complaints, lists

of what she did that deserved
better, and what better she
deserves. All day she nags
Hashem. He is the husband who
has to listen as she fills

his vast ear with sorrows.
He never shuts her up, so
her faith is a bright candle—
the fire in her marriage long
ago snuffed carelessly out.

Talking with my mother

"I don't believe in heaven or any of that
horseshit tied up with bows," she says.
"That's one advantage being Jewish,
among all the troubles I had: you don't
have to buy that nonsense. I'm just dead."

"Okay," I say, "but just suppose. Of your
three husbands, who would you want
waiting on the other side? Would they
line up? Would you have all three?"
"None," she says, "to hell with them.

I always remember the one I didn't
go off with. That's the one I would
think of when I lay awake beside
their snores. But likely he'd have turned
out the same. Piggy, cold, jealous,

self-occupied. Now that I'm dead
I don't have to worry I have no skills,
only worked as a chambermaid. No!
I'll live by myself in a clean house
with a cat or maybe two. Males.

Females are sluts. Like you," she
says, pointing. "I'll cook what I
like for a change—do the dead eat?"

"How would I know?" I ask. "Well,"
she says, "you're writing the dialogue.

I liked your poems, but the novels—
too much sex. In your books, too
much, in my last thirty years,
too little. Remember," she says, "you
never stop wanting it till you're dead.

No, I think I'll stay quiet. No more
money troubles, no more too fat,
too thin, no more of his contempt
and his sly relatives picking at me.
Let me go down into dirt and sleep."

Swear it

My mother swore ripely, inventively
a flashing storm of American and Yiddish
thundering onto my head and shoulders.
My father swore briefly, like an ax
descending on the nape of a sinner.

But all the relatives on my father's
side, gosh, they said, goldarnit.
What happened to those purveyors
of soft putty cussing, go to heck,
they would mutter, you son of a gun.

They had limbs instead of legs.
Privates encompassed everything
from bow to stern. They did
number one and number two
and eventually, perhaps, *it*.

It has always amazed me there are
words too potent to say to those
whose ears are tender as baby
lettuces—often those who label
us into narrow jars with salt and

vinegar, saying, People like *them*,
meaning me and mine. Never say
the K or N word, just quietly shut
and bolt the door. Just politely
insert your foot in the Other's face.

The streets of Detroit were lined with elms

I remember elm trees that were
the thing of beauty on grimy
smoke-bleared streets stinking of death
and garbage, but over the cramped
rotting houses, the elms arched.

They were cities of leaves.
I would lie under them
and my eyes would rise
buoyed up and surfeited
in immense rustling viridescence.

They enclosed me like a cathedral.
I entered them as into the heart
of a sanctuary in a mountain
pure and vast and safe.
I wanted to live in their boughs.

They gave no fruit, no nuts
and their fall color was weak,
but their embrace was strong.
I would stare at them, how
their powerful trunks burst

out of the dirt fully formed
and graceful, how they rushed

toward the sky and then halted
to spread out in a firmament
of green, of green, of green.

Dress up

Sleazy-thin as a too often washed
sort of white chenille bedspread,
curtains were wings or dancers'
costumes. In lopsided high heels

we clopped, posed twirling before
the mirror in some mother's off limits
bedroom we stole into, trying on
dresses now too tight on women

whose bellies hung where babies
had lodged again and again.
We never wanted to stay children
then. We wanted to drive away

in any car that offered a ride.
In the meantime we pocketed
lipsticks in the five and dime
tried on these dress up clothes

playing women we saw on Saturdays
at the picture show. We practiced
kissing and sometimes more
pretending to be a handsome man

who would offer us all we lacked.
We were desperate for more years—
tickets to escape on some elegant train
that would never stop here.

Minor street flooding is expected

In the Detroit of my childhood
after heavy rain, always the sewers
backed up into the basements,
always the storm drains clogged
and water filled the street,
an asphalt bottomed river.

Most likely it was filthy with germs
and garbage, that neighborhood
river, but what child of the inner
city cared? We had no pools,
no lakes. I never learned to swim.
But we waded among the cars

stranded like boulders, laughing,
splashing in shorts and turned up
jeans. We didn't care that basements
would be smeared with mud after
the waters crept out. This was our
river and we rolled in it like puppies.

So many pleasures we had were
accidental, a box discarded in an alley
with high heels we could hobble in,
a stray tabby become a pet, hard
furtive kisses against the wall
of a hallway smelling of cabbage.

Motown, Arsenal of Democracy

Fog used to bloom off the distant river
turning our streets strange, elongating
sounds and muffling others. The crack
of a gunshot softened.

The sky at night was a dull red:
a bonfire built of old creosote soaked
logs by the railroad tracks. A red
almost pink painted by factories—

that never stopped their roar
like traffic in canyons of New York.
But stop they did and fell down
ending dangerous jobs that paid.

We believed in our unions like some
trust in their priests. We believed
in Friday paychecks sure as
winter's ice curb-to-curb

where older boys could play
hockey dodging cars—wooden
pucks, sticks cracking wood
on wood. A man came home

with a new car and other men
would collect around it like ants
in sugar. Women clumped for showers—
wedding and baby—wakes, funerals

care for the man brought home
with a hole ripped in him, children
coughing. We all coughed in Detroit.
We woke at dawn to my father's hack.

That world is gone as a tableau
of wagon trains. Expressways carved
neighborhoods to shreds. Rich men
moved jobs south, then overseas.

Only the old anger lives there
bubbling up like chemicals dumped
seething now into the water
building now into the bones.

Portrait of the poet as a young nerd

At fourteen, at seventeen, at twenty-two
I chased myself through books.
I slipped into bodies of actresses,
mimicked their gestures, tried their smiles,
tilt of head, thrust of hip.

I could not find myself in any mirror.
I was not what I was supposed to be.
I did not look like anyone I saw.
My thoughts were weird as the monsters
superheroes killed in comic books.

As a girl I was a failure. I could
pick a lock but could not flirt.
Sports seemed pointless. Words
came easily, too easily, blabbing
me into tar pits of trouble.

I did not want to be a boy. Most
of them were imbeciles, I thought,
nor did I want to be a girl or woman.
Maybe I would grow up to be a cat.
Maybe I was an alien, a changeling.

I watched myself for extra powers—
the ability to read minds, to leap
tall buildings, to look through walls—
but found only a balky intelligence
and that slippery passion for words:

words talking in my head, words
building palaces along rusting
tracks of the Detroit Terminal Railroad.
Words had broader wings than pigeons,
bore the beaks and claws of eagles.

In the raw

How raw I am.
You find my words
give you heartburn
they are not easily
digestible although
they compost well.

I have sharp edges
some rusty
some glinting sharp.
You can't pick me
up safely to discard
or file securely.

I sprout porcupine
quills, cactus spines
cholla that can't be
brushed off but
irritate as they enter
your skin, your blood.

Women are not,
you say, supposed
to be wrought of flint

and recycled glass
of rich bottom mud
and fangs and bricks.

Oh, but we are.
We walk through the
valley of death
teeth chattering
and bared, ready
for fight or flight

or the strange
dangerous dance
of mating. I go
speaking myself again
and again like the cry
of a ravenous hawk.

Phantom pain

Three-layered cornbread, crisp and crusty
then hidden within, the tender custard:
I had not made it for a decade.

The recipe was given by a friend,
a gay man good in the kitchen.
We used to laugh ourselves limp,

shared dangerous afternoons, nights
streaked with political paranoia like
distant fires choking us with smoke.

That was before he began to view me
as a resource, someone from the other
side of the gender wars who could be used

now and then, but not trusted
any more than you trust a broken
board in a wooden bridge you inch across.

Behind me as I go are the torn
carcasses of murdered friendships, chest
cavities opened and the heart ripped out.

Pick a number

Between fear and numbness what do I dread?
The walls are closing like hands pressed together.
My heart is a clock; my blood slows to crude oil.
The clock is clogged and thinks of stopping.

Between faith and terror what do I guess?
The doors are all numbered out of order.
Behind each is something I never want.
Behind each is a separate shriek or moan.

Between sorrow and pity who do I love?
I walk quickly with my eyes closed
and each step waits for the void.
Between flight and freeze what devours me?

Between midnight and knife edge what do I beg
for, surcease or success, when do I stumble
into the answer I never want to hear
that tunnel into the earth of quiet bones.

Dislocation

It happens in an instant.
My grandma used to say
someone is walking on your grave.

It's that moment when your life
is suddenly strange to you
as someone else's coat

you have slipped on at a party
by accident, and it is far
too big or too tight for you.

Your life feels awkward, ill
fitting. You remember why you
came into this kitchen, but you

feel you don't belong here.
It scares you in a remote
numb way. You fear that you—

whatever *you* means, this mind,
this entity stuck into a name
like mercury dropped into water—

have lost the ability to enter your
self, a key that no longer works.
Perhaps you will be locked

out here forever peering in
at your body, if that self is really
what you are. If you *are* at all.

The closet of doom

Time to go through it all
clothes for which I am too big
clothes for which I am too small

How do these stains appear?
I swear I hung them clean. At night
do these dresses sneak like the twelve

princesses in the tale to a secret ball
to spill wine on their sleeves?
Snag their buttons on strange princes?

The fads of five years past embarrass
me. No one is wearing chartreuse
satin this year. Why did I fall

for the return of bell-bottoms?
So many mistakes arrayed on hangers.
If I had all that money spent, I could

buy something new that would soon
be too big, too small, spaghetti stained
quickly out of fashion. The resale shop

is already waiting for pants not yet
purchased, and I feel my own unplanned
obsolescence creep into my flesh.

The Hollywood haircut

I pay $35 to have my hair cut.
Last night I saw on television
from Hollywood a $400 haircut.

If I had a $400 haircut
would traffic part for me on the highway
like the Red Sea?

Would men one third my age
follow me panting in the street
and old men faint as I passed?

If I had a $400 haircut
would the rain stop
lest it dampen my perfect do?

If I had a $400 haircut
would my books become best
sellers and all my bills be written paid?

If I had a $400 haircut
would I have more orgasms—
louder ones. Would my eyelashes curl?

If I had a $400 haircut
would people buy calendars
just me on every month grinning?

If I had a $400 haircut
would everyone love me and
would you volunteer

to come clean my house
iron my never ironed shirts
and weed my jungle garden?

No? I thought so.
I'll stick to Sarah
and my $35 trim.

Minor characters

The people we think are walk-ons
in our major dramas, whose names
leak like tiny grains of couscous
through the sieve of our brains:

people who say hello in the drugstore
asking after our partners or pets
and we have no idea in hell
who they are and a weak smile

bubbles between our teeth
while we try to fake it: she's
the secret mistress of your loved
one who doesn't know her yet.

Then there's the guy in the woods
practicing with his .45 all
morning and with each shot
he sees your head explode.

You are incidental. He just
dislikes you enough to make
you number seven on his hit
list. A woman remembers how

when she asked, do you
like my whatever, a dress, a poem,
a speech, a dish of salmon loaf
you waited too long before you lied.

Behind us as we stroll uphill
and then down, crushed egos
like broken toys we stepped on
litter our steps. Somewhere

even now, a boy you insulted
in the supermarket is planning
to ruin you and drink your blood.
Best case: she has totally forgotten

your name and your face is pushed
from her mind by the force
of her genius, and you won't even
rate a footnote in her memoir.

In praise of joe

I love you hot
I love you iced and in a pinch
I will even consume you tepid.

Dark brown as wet bark of an apple tree,
dark as the waters flowing out of a spooky swamp
rich with tannin and smelling of thick life—

but you have your own scent that even
rising as steam kicks my brain into gear.
I drink you rancid out of vending machines,

I drink you at coffee bars for $6 a hit,
I drink you dribbling down my chin from a thermos
in cars, in stadiums, on the moonwashed beach.

Mornings you go off in my mouth like an electric
siren, radiating to my fingertips and toes.
You rattle my spine and buzz in my brain.

Whether latte, cappuccino, black or Greek
you keep me cooking, you keep me on line.
Without you, I would never get out of bed

but spend my life pressing the snooze
button. I would creep through wan days
in the form of a large shiny slug.

You waken in me the gift of speech when I
am dumb as a rock buried in damp earth.
It is you who make me human every dawn.
All my books are written with your ink.

The special one

I remember the boy on the rooftop
loosing his pigeons into the charred night sky
smeared with neon, rancid with soot,
the oven door of summer open on his face
and the birds a pastel banner flapping,
unfurling and tightening as they wheeled
as one body over East Harlem.

I remember a girl on a rooftop in Thessaloniki
feeding her doves, then letting them fly
up over the half crumbled ramparts where
steep crooked houses crouched against them,
the night, a deep dirty pocket of heat.
I heard her calling their names, half singing
Triandafilo, Handsome One, Star Chaser.

Sometimes on the Upper West Side of New York
in a pecking milling crowd of dirty grey pigeons
there struts a bird of spangled feathers,
a white dove, a bird crested or crowned,
a bird who took seriously the promise
of freedom tossed from its rooftop cage.

That boy who dreamed himself a drug
lord, big car, new house for his momma,
fine clothes and no bills that could not be paid
spat out his life in an alley among dog shit,
fast-food wrappers and empties.

That girl, pregnant by a boyfriend,
beaten by her brother, thrown out
by her father, died slowly of AIDS
in a narrow room under a roof where
a kid kept pigeons who cooed for her.
They were the last sound she heard
as her ears filled with blood, her doves
who rippled as one flock and returned,
but not the special one who got away.

The wind of saying

The words dance in the wind of saying.
They are leaves that crispen,
sere, turning to dust. As long
as that language runs its blood-

rich river through the tongues
of people, as long as grand
mothers weave the warp and woof
of old stories with bright new

words carpeting the air
into dreams, then the words
live like good bacteria
within our guts, feeding us.

We catch the letters and trap
them in books, pearlescent butterflies
pinned down. We fasten the letters
with nails to the white pages.

Most words dry finally to husks
even though dead languages
whisper, blown sand through
the dim corridors of library stacks.

Languages wither, languages
are arrested and die in prison,
stories are chopped off at the roots
like weeds, lullabies spill

on the floor and dry up.
Conquerors force their words
into the minds of their victims.
Our natural language is a scream.

Our natural language is a cry
rattling in the night. But tongues
are how we touch, how we reach,
how we teach, the spine of words.

How to Make Pesto

The good, the bad and the inconvenient

Gardening is often a measured cruelty:
what is to live and what is to be torn
up by its roots and flung on the compost
to rot and give its essence to new soil.

It is not only the weeds I seize.
I go down the row of new spinach—
their little bright Vs crowding—
and snatch every other, flinging

their little bodies just as healthy,
just as sound as their neighbors
but judged, by me, superfluous.
We all commit crimes too small

for us to measure, the ant soldiers
we stomp, whose only aim was to
protect, to feed their vast family.
It is I who decide which beetles

are "good" and which are "bad"
as if each is not whole in its kind.
We eat to live and so do they,
the locusts, the grasshoppers,

the flea beetles and aphids and slugs.
By bad I mean inconvenient. Nothing
we do is simple, without consequence
and each act is shadowed with death.

The orphan

I see all four cats lined up
on a level with the eastern windows.
I stand and there is a young deer

just six feet away staring at us
staring at him. It's December.
Why is he alone? He should still

be with his mother. Killed probably,
the shotgun season just ended.
But he has not learned to fear me.

He is fascinated by the cats and me
as he chomps rhododendron leaves.
I go right up to the window. Our eyes

meet, and still he does not run
but leisurely feeds, and I stay quiet
fearing for him, coyote food,

black powder season still to come.
He is exactly the color of Puck,
my blue Abyssinian, with eyes

big and shiny as blackberries.
Not until he is full does he turn,
white tail rising, and that's why

I say *he*. Finally then he is ready
to walk off stately as the buck
he will never become.

A long and busy night

Coyotes yelping in chorus after a kill
lick at the dark, raise my neck hair.
The moon in its clocktower of midnight
strikes the wood of bare trees.

How long is the night in winter
the snow brightening the ground
under a sky sootblack and thick.
The moon ignites every icicle

hanging their glass daggers
from the eaves. Then wind
gets up and turns, turns again
like a dog settling in a rough place.

Snow is coming in off the ocean.
We can feel heavy clouds
clotting now. The moon
is skimmed with grey ice.

The house creaks with cold,
and I can't sleep, wondering
what they killed, wondering
what bones the snow will cover

before morning seeps through
the swirling. I put on
the porch light to watch
flakes slant into oblivion.

In winter I wake to thoughts
of dying. At dawn, a red
tailed hawk dives on a junco
sits in the snow plucking

the feathers while winter
plucks at my flesh.

Buried

I have a passion for effigy mounds.
Once on tour I arranged for a night
in Prairie du Chien to see eagles, frogs.

The path up the cliff from the Mississippi
was icy. We crawled partway. And do
you know what an eagle mound looks like

under three feet of snow? Just like
that pile of stuff pushed to one side
of the parking lot at your local mall.

Snow conceals, muffles, shrouds.
Snow when it first falls makes even
ghetto streets clean, for half an hour.

A compost pile or a rock garden,
all the same. It erases roads.
How often have I gone out to shovel

and fallen off the porch into a drift.
Snow turns the landscape into secrets—
rusting radiators, the austere cathedral

skeleton of an arrow-shot deer only
a thaw gives up. All fallen—branches,
a tire, a red squirrel—buried together.

February ground

Three feet of snow in twenty-four hours
on top of seven inches. Not really
credible here. On the fourth day
we found the car under a six
foot drift and dug it out.

At first we could not open doors.
The post office shut for two days.
Our road had vanished into a field.
We felt the sky had finally
fallen and drowned us.

Six weeks: now patches of ground
emerge from white fortresses.
How beautiful is the dirt
I took for granted. Extraordinary
the wild green of grass islands.

Having the world snatched
from us makes us grateful even
for fence posts, for wheelbarrow
rising, for the stalwart spears
of daffodil uncovered.

Everything revealed is magical,
splendid in its ordinary shining.
The sun gives birth to rosebushes,
the myrtle, a snow shovel fallen,
overcome on the field of battle.

The stray

The sun places a hot hand on my skull
burning through my hair to exalt
the cold creases of my brain

much hotter than it will feel for months.
Open leaves cool us, but now
buds have not yet cracked to show

that slit of color, eye squinting
at the bright March world
marching to a snare drum into equinox.

Bark shines. Lavender crocuses are bent
double under the weight of hungry bees.
Everything is avid for spring.

The starving cat on the porch arches
into my hand, saying I survived
cold blasts and ice frozen in my

matted tail, coyotes and the great
horned owl, all hunting my flesh,
hiding under long Maine coon

black hair, as black as yours,
so I must belong to you. And so
he does, in spring, in order to live.

The month of aspirin

The month of aspirin, willow
the painkiller wisewomen used,
the month that overflows brooks
brings orgies of spring peepers
their high cries of ecstasy
chafing at the night.

Leaves unfurl damp flags.
Bees bend every crocus.
But willow is the first
tree to sprout and color:
chartreuse filaments
hanging their hair by the water

catkins fuzzy on branches.
The moon hides often
in grey clouds while eaves
drip monotone and the garden
drinks the rain, growing
while I watch, stretching.

One day the moon swells over
the sun, round as a basket
holding fire in its tight weave
a basket of willow wands
till the sun slides free.
Tonight in the moon's

quicksilver glow the willow
is pale as foam. The long
hair the wind sweeps to
and fro is almost white.
White as aspirin.
White as the moon's light.

More than enough

The first lily of June opens its red mouth.
All over the sand road where we walk
multiflora rose climbs trees cascading
white or pink blossoms, simple, intense
the scent drifting like colored mist.

The arrowwood is spreading its creamy
clumps of flower and the blackberries
are blooming in thickets. Season of
joy for the bee. The green will never
again be so green, so purely and lushly

new, grass lifting its wheaty seedheads
into the wind. Rich fresh wine
of June, we stagger into you smeared
with pollen, overcome as the turtle
laying her eggs in roadside sand.

Intense

One morning they are there
silken nets where the sun ignites
water drops to sparks of light—
handkerchiefs of bleached chiffon
spread over the grasses,
stretched among hog cranberry and heather.

Spiders weave them all at once
hatched and ready, brief splendor.
Walking to pick beans, I tear them.
I can't avoid their evanescent glitter.

I have never seen the little spinners
who make of my ragged lawn and meadow
an encampment of white tents
as if an army of tiny seraphim had deployed—
how beautiful are your tents O Israel—
the hand- or leggy-work of hungry spiders
extruding a tent city from swollen bellies.

How to make pesto

Go out in mid sunny morning
a day bright as a bluejay's back
after the dew has vanished
fading like the memory of a dream.

Go with scissors and basket.
Snip to encourage branching.
Never strip the basil plant
but fill the basket to overarching.

Take the biggest garlic cloves
and cut them in quarters to ease
off the paper that hides the ivory
tusk within. Grind Parmesan.

I use pine nuts. Olive oil
must be a virgin. I like Greek
or Sicilian. Now the aroma
fills first the nose, then the kitchen.

The UPS man in the street sniffs.
The neighbors complain; the cats
don't. We eat it on pasta, chicken,
on lamb, on beans, on salmon

and zucchini. We add it to salad
dressings. We rub it behind our
ears. We climb into a tub of pesto
giggling to make aromatic love.

Well done

The heat cooks the proteins of my brain
so that it can focus no better
than a heap of overcooked pasta.

The heat browns out the electricity
of my will so even crossing the room
to the bed seems a wearisome hike.

My thoughts have left me like dying
bats. My sex drive is reduced
to an almost inaudible whine.

Like an undertrained parrot
I have only one phrase to repeat:
it is hot, it is hot,

it is so very much too hot.
I lie in the mouth of the dog
of the days, half chewed.

Hurricane warning

The air weighs on you like a dead fish.
The sea has a look to it, expectant,
hungry, a tiger about to leap.
It very much wants to eat you.

Everything is too quiet. You
hear a dog barking
like a convulsive cough
across the marsh; a radio

announcing a Red Sox game;
hammering at a house site
two hills away. Your breath
clots in your nose like phlegm.

The paint of sweat sticks to skin.
You leave prints on what you touch.
The world around you is waiting
waiting for what will engulf it.

The weather is a jury still out.
In hurricanes, the wind is fate.
You almost long for what could
kill you, just to have done.

The moon as cat as peach

The moon is a white cat in a peach tree.
She is licking her silky fur
making herself perfect.

This is only a moment
round as a peach you have
not yet bitten into.

If you do not eat it,
it will rot. The peach
offers itself like a smile.

It cares only for the pit
hiding within. The cat
is waiting for prey.

She is indifferent
to the noisy boasting sun
that rattles like a truck

up the dawn sky clanging.
It is too early for such
clatter. She curls into sleep.

Tomorrow she will begin to hide
until you cannot see her
at all. She smiles.

August like lint in the lungs

If Jell-O could be hot, it would be this air.
Needles under the pines are bleached
to straw but mushrooms poke up white
yellow, red—wee beach umbrellas of poison.

Everything sags—oak leaf, tomato
plant, spiky candelabra of lilies,
papers, me. Sun burns acetylene.
Shade's a cave where dark waters bless.

Then on the radar of the Weather Channel
a red wave seeps toward us. Limp air
stiffens. Wind rushes over the house
tearing off leaves as the sky curdles.

The cat hides under the bed. We slam
windows and the door slams itself.
Everything is swirling as the army
of the rain advances toward us

flattening the tall grasses. Waves
break their knuckles on the roof.
Missiles of water pock the glass.
We feel under water and siege.

Then the rain stops suddenly
as if a great switch has been thrown.
Even the trees look dazed. Heat
creeps back in like a guilty dog.

Fagged out

Fagged out with fecundity,
the zucchini that thrust out
its cylinders like a green factory
lies limp as a pillow left out all
summer. It would pant if it could.

There is a point in the summer
when dying begins, even
while the grapes are coloring
and the pears still lengthening.
A hint of iron tinges the dawn.

Enough beaches and anti-
sun lotions slathered on dry skin;
enough faded cotton sundresses
wilted as dead lilies,
sneakers the ocean chewed.

The tomatoes are still round
and red as poppies, but
their leaves are yellowing.
Everything looks ragged
like a threadbare rug

and poking through is the earth
cool to the touch and ready
to receive the dying,
the dead and grind them up
into next year's fruit.

October nor'easter

Leaves rip from the trees
still green as rain scuds
off the ocean in broad grey
scimitars of water hard
as granite pebbles flung
in my face.

Sometimes my days are torn
from the calendar,
hardly touched and gone,
like leaves too fresh
still to fall littering
sodden on the bricks.

But I have had them—
torrents of days. Who
am I to complain they
shorten? I used them
hard, wore them out
and down, grabbed

at what chance offered.
If I stand stripped
and bare, my bones
still shine like opals
where love rubbed sweetly,
hard, against them.

The dawn of nothing

The foghorn moans in my sleep
I waken with the sense of something
gone wrong in the night

but it is only fog smothering
the house. Only fog
dissolving the pines.

A milky snake
has coiled itself around this island
and holds us stifling, still.

It swallows us. Digests us:
Oaks and picture windows,
pickup trucks and gazebo,

red fox and cottontail rabbit,
shed, winding road, grave.
This is visible solipsism.

No world lies beyond the white
curtain. Welcome to stasis,
welcome to the continuum

of blah. My eyes let it in.
My brain turns to vapor.
And the foghorn groans on.

Metamorphosis

On the folds of the cocoon
segmented, curled
like a little brown stairway
his fingers are gentle.

In the next chamber
he coaxes a newly hatched
green and purple caterpillar
onto a leaf, stroking it.

We all care for something,
someone. Maybe just our-
selves or family or money.
He loves butterflies.

He built a museum to them,
a sanctuary of fluttering.
Blue morphos, owl
eyes, cattle pinks, orange

and red and black,
umber, lemon, speckled
and zebra-striped
they zigzag around us.

Cold leans against the windows.
The roads are clogged
with ice, walled with old
grey snow like cement,

but here the air is warm
moist in our nostrils.
Flowers thicken it.
Now he is placing a cocoon

in a glass container
to change itself, hidden—
as if in a mummy case
an angel should form.

It will be a tobacco hornworm
moth, he says. *We pick
them off our tomato plants,*
Woody says, proud that we

never spray. The custodian
is shocked. *You can buy
tomatoes at the super-
market,* he says.

Not like ours, I say. A seed
the size of a freckle
turning into a five-foot
vine bearing red globes

big as my fist with
the true taste of summer
is miracle too: my garden's
yearly metamorphosis.

CHOOSE A COLOR

Choose a color

Between red and dead, we lived frightened
crouching, covering, signing loyalty oaths.
The war they called cold froze our brains.
The Russians were coming to burn
our flags and steal our color TVs.

Between green and machine, the ozone
fades away, scorching our flesh. Icecaps
seep into the sea. Hurricanes come
in quick posses. Drought or torrent.
BUSH: *We didn't know the levees could break.*

Between blue and Prozac, who will
you be? The brooks are grey with
antibiotics, antidepressants, pain
killers. The fish sleep upside down.
This pill will make you inane.

Between lavender and hellfire,
preachers froth. Get saved again,
again. Yet it still itches. In the
dark, what you really want licks
your thighs, burns hot in your brain.

Between white and night, dark
faces invade your entitlement.
They are stealing your birthright

to stomp and swell. Why can't
the world be peopled by only you?

Pick a color, any color from zero
to infinity, from blood to cancer,
from war to Armageddon, from AIDS
to bone, from here to no one
on a very fast jet.

Choices

Would you rather have health insurance
you can actually afford, or occupy Iraq?
Would you rather have enough inspectors
to keep your kids from getting poisoned
by bad hamburgers, or occupy Iraq?
Would you rather breathe clean air
and drink water free from pesticides
and upriver shit, or occupy Iraq?

We're the family in debt whose kids
need shoes and to go to the dentist
but we spend our cash on crack:
an explosion in our heads or many
on the TV, where's the bigger thrill?
It's money blowing up in those weird
green lights, money for safety,
money for schools and Head Start.

Oh, we love fetuses now, we even
dote on embryos the size of needle
tips; but people, who needs them?
Collateral damage. Babies, kids,
goats and alley cats, old women sewing,
old men praying, they've become smoke

blown away like sandstorms
of the precious desert covering treasure.

Let's go conquer more oil and dirty
the air and choke our lungs till
our insides look like stinky residue
in an old dumpster. More dead
people are obviously what we need,
some of theirs, some of ours. After
they're dead awhile, strip them
and it's hard to tell the difference.

Mighty big

A little arrogance is a dangerous thing
but a lot of arrogance is fatal
to children and kittens and countries.

To be sure you deserve all you can grab.
To be sure you can get away with it
because you hit harder and are willing

to strike the first blow: your opponent
lies dead at your feet, but guess what?
He had ten brothers and a wife who

can hit a thimble at a hundred yards.
He has children and grandchildren
who will be born with hatred for you

etched on their granite genes. Your
arches of triumph will stand in ten
years, monuments to empty victories

and history's last ironic chuckle.
You count and the rest don't
but someone is counting even now

the seconds to detonation. The harder
you push, the harder what you never
bothered to notice pushes back.

Security bottle

A rabid raccoon lurched
from the briars and swamp
azalea onto a neat lawn
in the next town

so today I go among
the pines and oaks
carrying little white bottles
of mountain lion piss

ordered from California.
The coyotes and raccoons,
it is written, will run
from the stink of this urine.

They will think among our
pussycats, we are harboring
a cat that would eat us all
or perhaps already has,

now aims to crunch
their bones. Rumors
of danger work as well
as the real thing for people

too, who will shed liberties
like motheaten sweaters
if they think that will
make them safe, whatever

safe is in a world busy
with Ebola, mad cow, dirty
bombs, suicide bombers,
nuclear waste, fast food

and other lethal entities
hungry to devour us
as our ancestors ran
from cave bears, saber

toothed tigers and fevers
that swarmed from the water.
This world offers no safety
to worm, to raccoon, to us.

Counting the after-math

People penned to die in our instant
concentration camps, just add water,
bodies pushed to the side.

Thirst hurts worse than hunger.
It swells your brain against your skull.
It sandpapers your gut from within.

But hunger too makes people crazy.
Shoot the looters who are grabbing
from flooded stores survival for hours more.

Baby is crying
Grandma is dying
and that dirty water is getting higher

Talk to the camera about why didn't these
crazy people evacuate? Without cars,
without money, without credit cards—

why didn't they fly away like gulls?
Why didn't they get on their yacht
and chug upstream? But even at the Ritz

when they ran out of food and water
the manager told tourists to "find"
food in the deserted stores.

Baby is crying
Grandma is dying
and that dirty water is getting higher

All the cats climbing the rafters
their fur sodden with stinking refuse
laden water and drowning.

All the dogs chained to porches
as the water rose, swimming in
narrowing circles. FEMA says

we didn't know about the thousands
in the convention center, as millions
saw them on TV screaming for help.

Baby is crying softer now
Grandma is up to her chin
and that dirty water is still getting higher

Who will count the bloated bodies?
Who will weep for children silenced?
For mothers drifting like belly-up goldfish?

Who will mourn that African-American town
corrupted by the rich, enriched by the poor
with spicy music and mama's sexy cooking?

Baby has stopped crying
Grandma has drowned
and that dirty water is still getting higher.

Your proper place

Get back in the box. It's
a nice box, pink, cozy.
Lined with quilted satin.
It smells of carnations, lavender.

It's a box with a view:
tidy white streets lined
with trim white houses housing
nice white people.

There's a church on every
block with a phallic steeple
where God the Father is
worshipped and sin exposed.

Everything you need to know
is contained in a little book
about Dick and Jane and Spot.
Spot chases a bitch and goes

straight to hell. So does she
with other wicked females.
But you're safe: just so long
as you stay in your box.

Rotten

I was seventeen, just hired
by Michigan Bell to work the switchboard
inhabited by giant cockroaches.

The company sent me to the dentist,
I don't know why. My parents
had never bothered with one.

He looked into my mouth, my teeth
rotted by sugary diet, and said
How much money you got?

Fifteen dollars. *Okay, then I*
pull them. Fillings cost more.
I was seventeen. He yanked out

three molars and I went bleeding
home on the Livernois bus.
The taste of my blood

was thick in my mouth.
We were used to the butt
end of things, us Detroit

kids with our anger and our
scars, we were used to being
pissed on, but we minded.

Tanks in the streets

Tanks that year in the streets
lined with bosomy elms—
tanks with slowly turning turrets
like huge dinosaur heads
their slitted gaze staring us down
soldiers with rifles sheltered
in their arms like babies
stalking past the corner drugstore.

They were entering a foreign land
occupied by dangerous natives:
Detroit: a pool of rainbow
slithering oil ringed by suburbs
of brick colonials and ranches,
then the vast half hidden
fortified houses of those who
grew rich off Detroit.

Class hatred was ground into
my palms like grease into
my brother's hands, like coal
dust into my uncle's. TV
had not yet taught us we
were nothing and only
celebrities had lives that
counted. We poured into

the streets, but the ones we
struck with our rocks, bottles,
were each other, white against
Black, Polack against Jew,
Irish against hillbilly. Always,
after the tanks rolled off
it was our corpses strewn
in every riot, in every war.

Sur l'ile Saint Louis

The past superimposes, palimpsest.
We are staying in a small pleasant
hotel, blue tiled courtyard. We take
our morning café au lait in bed.

In the evenings we grab takeout
from one of fifty places the working
affluent pick up their suppers.
All is pretty, benign here in the center

of the Seine, looking at the back
side of Notre Dame, the park
where gay men cruise each other.
We eat pomegranate ices by the river.

In '57 this was a monstrous slum
shown me by my soon-to-be-hus-
band to prove Paris could be worse
than my Detroit, and it sort of was.

Stench of sewage, toilets oozing
streams of shit across the pavement
stones, all under a great sunburst
bas relief on the far courtyard wall.

A kid in dirty throwaways
was picking through garbage bins

in desperate search. A runover dog
lay unregarded in the narrow street.

My fiancé's mother hid him here
blocks from the old ghetto, waiting
to flee into the mountains, to cross
the barbed border to Switzerland.

This visit, I'm researching the revolution:
Manon's house, small footsteps
of hope and horror, Danton trying
to speak as they readied his beheading.

History stalks me as I search for it.
My eyes cannot help seeing
its shadows under every lamppost,
its shape misshaping my life.

Deadlocked wedlock

Marriage is one man and one woman
they say, one at a time, then another, another.
You see the buffed faces of old men shining
with money as they lead their young blonds
and toddlers, second or third families,
the shopworn wives donated to Goodwill.

It has always been so, they say,
one man and one woman in the Bible—
like Jacob with Leah and Rachel
and the bondmaidens dropping children
his four women competing to swell
like a galaxy of moons.

In Tibet women had various husbands at once.
I had two myself for a few years.
In earlier times and different cultures
and tribes, men married men and women
married women, and the sky never fell.
People loved as they would and must

and the rivers still ran clean and the grass
grew a lot harder and more abundantly
than it does for us. What damage

does love do in the soft grey evenings
when the rain drifts like pigeon feathers
across the sky and into the trees?

Why, gentlemen, do you fear two women
who walk holding hands with their child?
Two fifty-year-old men exchange rings
and kiss, and you catch mad cow disease
as fallout? What do you hate when you
watch lovers? What are you really missing?

National monument: Castle Clinton

Castle Garden was America's point of entry for immigrants between 1850 and
1890, before Ellis Island was opened.

Robert Moses wanted to tear it down.
He was good at that. But history
buffs mobilized. It was restored:

to what? The 1812 fort. Just
what we all need, an unimportant
military position, walls and cannons:

Castle Clinton as a bloodless ring
of stones staring at rough grey
water attacked only by gulls.

Eight million people trekked through
Castle Garden with rough bundles of hope,
ragged with fear and hunger, children

clutching their mother's drugget skirts,
a procession of shawls bowed down
by whatever they could carry or drag

disgorged into a park where dapper
folks listening to a band play marches
glared. They were set upon like quail

by a pack of snapping dogs—recruiters,
boardinghouse and brothel keepers,
those looking for the cheapest

labor they could wring work from.
Eight million staggering ashore
from steerage, danger nipping

at their heels, trail of blood.
No, that would be a dismal monument,
monument to sweat and dirty rags

monument to real bony forebears
who suffered to arrive, shoved
out those massive doors into a city

waiting with iron teeth to chew them.

I met a woman who wasn't there

The CIA should hire as spies
only women over fifty, because
we are the truly invisible.

We pass through checkpoints
as if through spiderwebs
with only a slime of derision.

Watch television, go to
the movies: you see men of all
ages, children, young females.

Older men thrive with escorts
half their age, but older
women must die off en masse.

In middle age, even with Botox,
liposuction, face lifts, tummy
tucks, whatever mad torture

to the poor hardworking flesh
surgeons can devise, we
begin to vanish. Walk through

a lobby, a crowded airport:
men, children will run into you
in the obvious opinion you

cannot possibly exist. We
are inaudible too. We speak
and people turn away. Although

we know much, our opinions
are dust on the wind. Nobody
collects or records them.

We are the age's lepers, preferably
penned out of sight in colonies
of hunger. *You have let your-*

self go. You have not refused
the years politely, firmly like an
anorexic at a dinner party.

History's warnings are etched
on our bones. Like Cassandra
we have witnessed wars and famines

and foresee that wind of ash
blowing in, but to our prophecies
only our cats will listen.

Morning's e-mail

Enlarge your penis
by five inches
to satisfy "her"
while traveling to Cancún
on the cheap
paid for by a second
mortgage on your home
even with bad
credit history
and no job.

Here are ten
eye-burning stock tips.
Lose twenty pounds
with our pill.
Sign up for our
at home business
and earn millions
in your sleep.
Small fee required.
Get Viagra for pennies.

I am a businessman
in Nigeria with millions
to deposit in your name.
Good faith fee required.
Hot teenage nude girls

panting for you.
Sign up here. Just
fill in our form,
social security number.

A sucker taken
hook on line
and sunk.

Absolutely safe

Take the pills, little lady, take the pills
once daily, they will keep far away
those vampires of stroke and heart attack
that sucked the life from your mother,

that killed your brother. You will sleep
better. Look in the mirror at you:
younger, softer, sweeter, more content.
Just buy and swallow your pills, O woman

of a doubtful and dubious age, woman
who matters little to drug megacorps
who is a cow to be milked, a cow
to be coaxed up the gangway

in the reek of spilled and stale blood.
Of course they're safe, we tested them,
read the medical journals. Doctors
line up in chorus to sing how they will

make you healthier, saner, smarter,
stronger. You need them, your body
is addicted to them now, craves
estrogen as once it sucked nicotine.

Breaking news: we were wrong, ladies,
These magic pills don't prevent strokes,

they cause them. Our bad. Or yours.
They won't cure you after all

of age and pain and waste and trouble.
They won't cure but might kill you
perhaps with breast cancer. But
who that really matters really cares?

Next week we will release a new study
funded by a pharmaceutical company
to prove arsenic builds strong bones
and a new pill grows hair on toads.

Money is one of those things

Money is one of those things like health:
when you have it you feel entitled.
It's part of you like your left elbow
or your front teeth. But they can

easily be pulled and so can your
credit, your wage, all that money
you squirreled away in the stocks
going up like rockets on the Fourth.

Money never belongs to us.
It's a paper fiction we believe
like the first guy who says
in the backseat he loves you.

He's already planning a move
on a cheerleader, but his voice trembles
a little and you're too young to
know it's his hard-on talking.

Money comes on that way. You
want that, it tells you, you got to have
a new couch, a new car, a new nose.
I'll make you so happy, it croons,

I'll make you shine like a gas fire
burning in a car that just rear-ended

an SUV, and don't you want one too?
I love you, I'm yours forever

money sings, you're so important
unique, I'm your love slave.
Just make a central place for me
in your heart, your hearth. Right

there where your brain used to be.
Oh, it comes and it goes like a tide
pulled by a titanium moon, and what
it truly loves and obeys is power.

Less than you bargained for

New bargains every day
in our packed aisles, come on!
Trappist jams, lamps in the form
of Buddhas, striped baskets,
ceramic bowls of potpourri
that will never scent a room
after the first five minutes.

All the gifts you buy friends
who thank you profusely
before stowing them in a closet
or taking them to the dump
the next week. The detritus
of busted capitalism, shops,
businesses gone belly up,

of sweatshops in Guam
making baskets for a nickel.
This is the bizarre bazaar
of knickknacks nobody truly
wants—bargains galore.
Everything you don't need
at prices you can afford.

White night

This is the place they know you
by the paper bracelet on your wrist.
This is the place you are wakened
at 5 a.m. for a sleeping pill.
This is the place six doctors
stand over you as if you were
a platter of turkey and discuss
how to carve you.

This is the place they take
from you your clothes, your
dignity, your name. Like a child
you are Marge and only doctors
have surnames and power.
This is the place you are not
supposed to read your records
or understand the pills they
hand you with a minute cup
of water.

This is the place that smells
of antiseptic but blood floats
in the air ducts and pain
is bright and white and no
one apparently can see it

but you as it picks you up
in its teeth and chews
you to pulp.

This is the place ruled by
insurance companies, by suits
who know only spreadsheets
and dividends. This is the place
people are told of "discomfort"
while all night they scream.
This is the place I do
not want to go. This
is no place to live
or to die.

Buyer beware

If you subscribe to a magazine about dogs,
It comes full of canine advice and pictures. Woof.
If you buy a winter coat, you can reasonably
count on its being warmer than your bare skin.
If you buy a pig in a poke, it should oink at least.
What do you get when you buy a war?

Trillions of dollars in debt, for one thing.
Every grenade that explodes, ka ching ka ching.
Every ordnance, every vehicle, every plane:
see the smoke rising? That's money on fire.
That's your taxes at work. Does it help you?
Is it better than repairing the local bridge

you drive across every commuting morning?
Is it better than putting kids through college
so they aren't motivated to steal your car?
Is it better than having health insurance
that actually pays your hospital bills entire?
Is it nicer than cleaning up the air you breathe

or equipping miners so they don't die
by the dozen down there in the smoky dark.
What do you get when you buy a war?
Security? No, the country you invade

is chock full of people who now hate you.
They're dying to invade you back.

Shopping is our favorite entertainment.
We go to the mall to wander and eyeball
stuff. More stuff. We're stuffed with stuff.
But at least you can wear that orange
cashmere sweater. You can gobble that pizza.
What do you get when you buy a war?

Death. You get death retail and whole-
sale. You get death by the planeload.
You get young death, old death, baby
death. You get part death—limbs blown
off, heads racked with shrapnel, spines
torn apart and brains toasted. Theirs

and ours. You are delivered mistrust
and hatred by the decadeload. You
purchase rape and pillage, you purchase
torture and graft, bribery and looting.
Your great-grandchildren will pay off the debt.
Are you happy with your purchase of this war?

Sneak and peek

Under the Patriot Act, any strong arm
of law enforcement
has the right to enter your home covertly
while you sleep
while you are out
under suspicion you might
be hiding something under the bed
among your boxers or thongs
on your computer among the porn.

Are you patriotic?
Do you submit lists of what you read
to the FBI without waiting to be asked?
Do you spy on your neighbors checking
if they play Middle Eastern music
if they smoke other than tobacco
if they read the wrong books—all u.s.
right thinking people know what
they are. If they have too much sex
or sex of the wrong kind—all u.s.
right thinking people know exactly
what we mean. Do you believe
in the separation of Church and Hate?
Evil our president says is everywhere
and obvious and must be invaded
mostly by workingclass kids
whose morality is dubious anyway
unless they die as heroes.

We, your bornagain FBI
have collected receipts from your
restaurant meals for the past five years.
You have ordered hummus six times,
falafel twice and lamb four times
which is suspect because your
president eats only beef and ham.
What are you planning to do with that
sesame tahini from Stop & Slop?

You have turned off the television
48 times while Our President spoke
words of wisdom and Christian endeavor.
During the State of the Union address
you were observed on your couch
making derogatory faces and obscene
remarks. You have e-mailed quotes
from our sacred leader miscalling
him Shrub. You may not criticize
the president nor his lady Laura
nor his omniscient veep
the great grey Cheney of oil
nor the secretary of defense
Our Donald whose brain shines
bright as solid titanium
or our Grand Master Gonzales
into whose perked up ears
every men's and women's

room in the country is directly
bugged. You may be detained
on suspicion of being suspicious.
You want to protest?
That's grounds enough.
You are under arrest.
You have no right to remain
silent, to seek counsel
or to defend yourself. Welcome
to the New Inquisition.

In our name

In your name we have invaded
come with planes, tanks and artillery
into a country and wonder why
they do not like us
be proud

In your name we have bombed villages
and towns and left torn babies,
the bloated bellies of their mothers,
a little boy crying for his father
who lies under his broken house
the smashed arms of teenagers
in the sunbaked streets
every death creates a warrior
be proud

In your name we have taken men
and women from their homes
in the afternoon breaking down their doors
in the night waking them to the rattle
of weapons leaving their children
weeping with fear
be proud

In our name we have taken those we suspect
because they were in the wrong place
or because someone who hated them gave their names

or because a soldier didn't like the way they stared at him
put them in cells and strung them up like slaughtered cattle
stripped their clothes and mocked them naked
ran electricity through their tender parts
set dogs to rip their flesh
in your name
be proud

This is who we are becoming.
There is none other but us sanctioning this.
In our name young boys from Newark and Sandusky
are shot at by people who live in the place
they have been marched to.
In our name a young woman from Detroit
is disemboweled by a bomb.
In our name the sons of out of work miners
step on land mines.
In our name their bodies are shipped home.
In our name fathers return to their children
maimed and blind, their brains seared.

This is who we are in Athens or in Lima not Ohio
when people glare at us in the street.
This is the person my passport identifies,
the one who allows the order to be given
for blood to be mixed with sand
for bones to be mixed with mud

In our name is all this being carried out right now
as we sit here, as we speak, as we sleep.
Every day we do not act, we are permitting.
Every day we do not say no, we all say yes
be proud.

MATING

In St. Mawes

Rooks were guffawing outside in the oaks
and I ran out to look at their colony,
a word from chess now feathered, black, shining
in their effrontery and communal games.

The house was white columned regency:
a stairway that rose like a perfect scale
sung by a soprano with silver voice.
We had the best room Byron slept in.

That evening I seduced him successfully
for the first time in three months.
I thought it was renewal. It was the last
throes, a final rite of no passage.

I suckled hope from his mouth,
I gathered him into me to be reborn
as my lover, my best friend, my peer
but the rooks had the unity I craved.

In the morning's mist grey light
he was angry I had broken through.
He put on armor of pique. Nits
swirled to be picked and pickled—

always nits can be found under pillows
in the underwear drawer, tucked in
a passport. I made love with the death
of love while the rooks jeered.

Not knowing what I know

A cheap hotel in Blois
where we could hear the whores
and their johns through thin
walls rank with peeling paper,
a sink in the room stained
turquoise by dripping.

All day we had hitchhiked
in the rain, sharing a baguette
going stale, chocolate, an orange.
A trucker finally picked us up
his huge red hand crawling
across my thigh. You didn't notice.

In that wheezing bed I held
you, shuddering with the night
mare of torture you would
not relate. As the whores
made loud noises of
nonpleasure, I knew

there in bedbug bitten dark
you would not love me.
With dawn I forgot. Once
again I blew warm breath
on cold ashes, still sure
I could make fire.

The young and the stupid

So passionate, possessed,
dragging her ass across the carpet,
bellowing her need like a dramatic
mezzo-soprano in a solo opera,
Efi is too young for what she endures.

Only four months old, she would
die of sex if she were let out
through the crack in the door
she sniffs eagerly, a strange
rakish tom outside winking

at her from under the winter
roughened rhododendron.
She begs for her fate, rolling
tiny belly up with nipples
pink and distended.

When I watch her, it is not
a kitten I see but a girl,
myself, my girlfriend, my shadow
pursuing sulky spiteful Heathcliff
in any handmedown guise,

studying the best and chasing
the worst into its bed of spikes.
Leaping into the bonfire singing
it must be love, it must be
love because it hurts.

Many, many loves

So many things we can love:
a man, a woman, a friend, a cat.
We can love a sugar maple
turning orange from the bottom up;
we can love a weeping beech
with its twisting arms, the lush tent
branches make sweeping the ground.

We can love a pond, a shore, a boat.
We can love a painting, a flag,
abstractions like honor and country.
We can love icons and temples.
A house, a yard, a woods, a path
that leads us wandering toward
the place we'd most like to be.

Some can love a car—I never could—
a book, a doll, a necklace or ring.
Some can love family and some can't.
Some—the luckiest—can love
themselves without narcissism
just saying, *Well, I am this, I could
do better now and probably I will.*

Bashert*

Remember when you invited me into
your kitchen and cut a ripe mango:
orange, deep scented, juicy on a green
platter. I thought then, perhaps
we will be lovers.

Remember when you came up the gravel
drive and I fed you my grandmother's
sour cherry soup, cold and touched
with cream. You wondered
then, could we be lovers?

So many years worn away, smoothed
in the swift waters of memory.
Suppose you had not driven out
that June day, suppose it had rained
suppose I had accepted a former

lover's Iowa invitation. Suppose,
a hundred forking divergent moments
like the intricate web of a broken
windshield. Or maybe the dividing
paths of a myriad other choices

would have joined back to the master
trunk where we clasp each other

*the destined one

murmuring love. I was the juicy
mango you bit into that day, and you
are my sweet and my sour

my past and my future, my best
hope and my worst fear, my friend
and brother and sparring partner.
Chance or fate, we grasped what
was offered us and we hold on.

Bread dreams

The slow rise of the dough
is a breast forming on a young
girl, as if we were watching years
ripen her body.

The yeasty smell's a bit like sex,
a little like fruit. The seeds
wink from dough the color
of chocolate milk. The seeds

are slender as black crescent
moons but as many as stars.
I bite down hard on a caraway
to devour its sharp savor.

I bury my hands in the dough
and then slap it, bang it,
divide it only to marry it
to itself, punched down.

Now I am folding it over and
over. I imagine sleeping
in warm dough. I imagine
I'm kneaded into it to dream

oh, soundly, sweetly, with
seeds in my hair. I rise,
I enlarge, I am four times
what I was and ready to bake.

Train from Nice

Sitting in the compartment
of an all night train from Nice
to Paris, we stared at the moon
icing the olive trees, the wheat
fields, and suddenly we rode
through van Gogh's eyes.

We did not sleep, gliding
through cities we could not
identify, making love
awkwardly in the tiny
space, jarred apart
slammed together.

We were new at marriage
still with too many elbows,
apologies, demands
thrown down like a poker
hand that is sure to lose—
the bluff, failed.

We were killing time gladly
wandering before a noon
plane home from de Gaulle,
a morning strolling narrow
streets through the grey Marais
in the near hallucinatory

glare of sleep deprivation
yet even yawning, spinning
on nothing but caffeine,
I saw then we had come
through; that trust had
woven a net of new

arteries threading our
flesh. We had begun
to speak through silences
like a night landscape
the moon makes visible
showing us our new strait path.

Famous lovers stumbled upon

In Père-Lachaise on a yellow
November afternoon, leaves
wet with last night's rain
we found by chance the tomb
of Heloïse and Abelard.

I was startled. It was
as if we had found
the graves of Tristan
and Yseult. Literary
myth had real bones.

So she really suffered
and he really bled.
What a strange afterlife
for those not altogether
forgotten, to become

a story, a song like Barbara
Allen, all the flesh
cooked from the skeleton
simplified into a shape
nothing like our fat lives.

The house is empty

The house is empty as a cast up shell
whitened on the beach among debris
of bleach bottles, skate egg holders,
bladderwrack the waves abandoned—
a shell rubbed thin, shining
like a moon disc.

The moon is barren except
for astronauts' garbage. The house
is empty of you. I wander
through the days and rooms
of absence, I root in the bed
for the scent of your body.

Tasks fill the hours but still
they rattle, the dry seeds
of the minutes warning me
snakelike that all presence
is temporary. Why do we
waste any of the thinning

time apart? Let us join
at the hip on midnight's cusp
our blood singing anthems.
Let's praise every meal shared,
every wine savored, every
kiss, every fuck, every

handclasp and each conversation
that is not a quarrel.
Pull the covers up over
our sated bodies tonight
and let our sleep be melded
into one dream, hooked together.

The lived in look

My second mother-in-law had white carpeting
white sofa with blue designer touches.
Everything sparkled. Walking on the beach
I got tar on bare feet. Footprints

across that arctic expanse marred
perfection. I have never eaten
without dribbles and droplets exploding
from me like wet sparks on tablecloth

on my clothes, on the ceiling,
miraculously appearing five blocks
away as stigmata on statues. In short
a certain limited chaos exudes from

my pores. Everyone over fifty was born
to a world where ideal housewives
scrubbed floors to blinding gloss
in pearls and taffeta dresses on TV.

Women came with umbilical cords
leading to vacuum cleaners. You
plugged in a wife and she began
a wash cycle while her eyes spun.

Every three weeks we shovel out
the kitchen and bath. Spanish moss

of webs festoon our rafters. Cat hair
is the decorating theme of our couches.

Don't apologize for walls children
drew robots on, don't blush for last
month's newspapers on the coffee
table under cartons from Sunday's takeout.

This is the sweet imprint of your life
and loves upon the rumpled sheets
of your days. Relax. Breathe deeply.
Mess will make us free.

Making love new

Married love is remaking,
rekindling, taking this lump of
light at the center of our beings
and feeding it bright, blinding
again, the spine like an elon-
gated hot coal liquefying
the cold gelid brain.

Some sex is for pleasure,
some for expressing love.
Some sex is for reknitting
what sharp words have torn,
some is a blanket thrown
over a shivering child, some
a promise, we will continue.

Unpaid bills, insults, sickness,
political struggles swarm
the bed, mosquitoes drawing
blood and attention. Married
sex is a discipline more
focused than yoga: making
love new the ten thousandth time.

Hot heart

The fire in the fireplace
mutters and then sings
and sometimes snaps
loud and sudden
as a window breaking
coughing up sparks.

The fire is tamed
but its song is of
eating the house,
drinking trees to ash,
slaking its wild thirst
on all living and dead.

Blue, green, orange
how it dances
lapping along the logs.
The cats stare into
its roaring heart
danger whistling

up the chimney:
wolf tamed to dog
all wild instincts
intact. Desire banked
in the marriage bed
erupting but contained.

Falling uphill

Love is half luck and half work.
You fall into it, people say—
tripping uphill into a place
you always dreamed of.

The first day or week or year
you bite into each other like
ripe plums, all juice and savor.
The pit just centers your desire.

Later you notice the way
he chews his food. He observes
how your long hair drifts
like cobwebs through the house.

He finds a long black one
snaking through the soup. After
that it's either working into bliss
or stomping off to go hunting.

But there is a point way, way
uphill when you pause and look
at him and say, yes, this
is it, what I am going to know

of love before I fall to dust.
This man is fate, my nubbly
half, the answer to my young
questions. He is the face

of my beloved that I must
kiss with my heart in my throat
take into me with joy and caring
and care for come fire, come high

water, come lightning and hail
and plagues of locusts and
governments collapsing on us:
we are coupled till death.

At the core of loving, fear

I fear the government, lightning, car crashes.
I fear food poisoning, fire, coyotes.
I fear war, the hatred of women, of Jews.
I fear blindness and cancer and ticks.

But the fear that intertwines my spine
creeping from belly to brain—
a poison ivy vine circling an oak—
is to outlive you and march grimly on.

The terror at the core of every long
and bone deep love is that I may
survive into the empty rooms,
nights of neglect and dusty throat

parched from too much silence,
loneliness eating me hollow the way
tiny parasitic wasps hatch to devour
a hornworm from the inside.

I feel myself doomed as a caterpillar
who subsists on the leaf of a single
plant and that rare and threatened.
You are my daily bread and joy.

We are so intertangled that pulling
one away leaves not a single person
but a part, for we together make a whole
greater than the sum of our hearts.

Mated

You are shoveling snow in the long drive
down to the road, tossing it. From
my window you resemble a great
downcoated bear shaking himself dry.

You cannot make a good omelet;
I cannot fence the tomato garden.
You cannot balance a checkbook;
I cannot pull out a rusted screw.

I can make perfect pie dough; you
can plow all the gardens by dusk.
I can speak French and Spanish,
learn languages enough to manage

Czech, Greek, Norwegian, what
ever travel requires; you can drive
on the wrong side of roads, conquer
roundabouts an hour out of Heathrow.

I can read maps; you read spread-
sheets, wiring diagrams. That's
what mating is, the inserting of
parts that together make completion

prick and cunt, word and answer
all the antiphony of love.

The poetry of flesh

If you were a cabbage, my love
you would be a big red spicy one
a touch of hot in the wet and crunchy.

If you were a tree, my love
you would be a sugar maple
with sap of honey and flaming leaves.

If you were a sea creature, my love
you would leap hotblooded from the waves
grinning and rescue swimmers.

A pot roast braised in red wine
with sweet carrots melting in the mouth.
Home churned peach ice cream

with bits of fruit on a humid night.
A rum baba. A bombe of a peony
so rich in scent it stains the air.

A fiord glimmering with waterfalls
galloping down the steep rocks.
A morning in the high desert

after rain when every cactus
and thornbush explodes into flowers
and the hummingbirds hover whirring.

I turn you into a flood of metaphors
piled on each other to toppling.
Still nothing suffices but you.

The mystery of survival

So much feels arbitrary. How could
I know that August afternoon when
a hawk rose from its torn rabbit
in the bayberries that I would set down
deep scrabbling roots in this hillside?

So I gouged a furrow in this hill
for a drive upward and a hole for a house
wedged into the sand and clay. I planted
trees now huge that look like forever.
Weeds and lilies and green bridal

bouquets of broccoli pour from my
fingers sunk in soil made from garbage
from mulch of salt hay and thatch.
Born in Detroit's smoking ghetto
how do I come to be planted by a marsh

where redwinged blackbirds nest
where the great horned owl raises
February owlets in a storm blasted
oak? The man I came here with
left with an heiress one bleak winter.

Many came, many went. The hill
gave me blueberries and poison
ivy. The hill gave me home. How
many countries I hitchhiked over,
cities where I camped in rooms

cockroaches and corrupt landlords
owned. Smoke was the color I knew.
The smell of urine soaked hallways,
cabbagey, lit by a flickering bulb.
How did I come to my green garden

of labor and love? This land
is my only security. We do
money dances but it seldom
rains on us. I squandered years,
embraced gaunt scarecrows of desire,

mad dogs of anger, sullen children
with beards—I immolated myself.
My life zigzagged and sped through
pain, a rollercoaster on crack.
Now here I am planted like one

of my oaks. I build ziggurats
of words, but I am rooted in earth
deep, drinking the hidden waters.
Our roots are braided and love
like minerals flows between.

Is this accidental or inevitable?
In parallel worlds I bleed to death
pregnant at eighteen; in the mirror
world I rot in prison; I am stymied
in grey spiderwebs of despair.

There I call and the wall answers.
Here our words twine like roses
climbing red and robust on the arbor
you built. We map our lives toward
this house, this hour—every lesson

learned, every mistake a step up.
But this summer a hurricane could
level the house. Cancer could burrow,
its busy cells like fire ants swarming.
Bumper cars on the highway at 70.

We craft what sense we can
out of the maelstrom. We transmute
our buffeting, our swirling plunging
ricochets into a dance, forcing
good and bad luck into destiny.

THE BIRTHDAY OF
THE WORLD

My grandmother's song

We were girls, said my grandmother.
We went to the river with our laundry
we beat on the stones, washing
it clean, and then we spread it
on the wide grey boulders to dry.

We were laughing, said my grandmother
all of us girls together unmarried
and mostly unafraid, although of course
as Jews we were always a little on edge.
You know how a sparrow pecks seeds

always watching, listening for danger
to pounce. We gossiped about bad
girls over the river and boys and who
had peeked at us as we passed.
We took off our clothes, hung them

on bushes and bathed in the cool
rushing water, telling of Maidele
who threw herself in the current
to carry her big belly away, telling
of ghosts and dybbuks, of promises.

Then my Grandmother would sigh and dab
a small tear, and I would wonder
what she missed. I would rather
bathe in a tub, I said, in warm water.
The mikvah was warm, she said, and

the river was cold, but we liked
the river, young girls who did not
guess what would happen to us, how
our hopes would melt like candlewax
how we would bear and bear children

like apples falling from the tree
so many, but a tree that bled
and some would just rot in the grass.
You never forget the ones who die,
she said, even if you held them only

two months or twelve, they come
back in the night and circle like fish
opening silent mouths and never
do they grow older, but you do.
Your hair hangs like strands

of a worn out mop, your flesh
puffs up like bread from too much yeast
or dwindles till your arms are brittle
sticks and the frost never leaves you.
I want to go down to the river

again, I want to hear the singing
and tell stories with friends we would
never tell in front of our mothers.
I want to go down to the river,
wade in and let it wash my bones

down to the hope that must surely
still form their marrow, deep
and rich in spite of the sights
that have dimmed my eyes
and tears that have pickled my heart.

The late year

I like Rosh Hashonah late,
when the leaves are half burnt
umber and scarlet, when sunset
marks the horizon with slow fire
and the black silhouettes
of migrating birds perch
on the wires davening.

I like Rosh Hashonah late
when all living are counting
their days toward death
or sleep or the putting by
of what will sustain them—
when the cold whose tendrils
translucent as a jellyfish

and with a hidden sting
just brush our faces
at twilight. The threat
of frost, a premonition
a warning, a whisper
whose words we cannot
yet decipher but will.

I repent better in the waning
season when the blood
runs swiftly and all creatures

look keenly about them
for quickening danger.
Then I study the rockface
of my life, its granite pitted

and pocked and pickaxed
eroded, discolored by sun
and wind and rain—
my rock emerging
from the veil of greenery
to be mapped, to be
examined, to be judged.

The birthday of the world

On the birthday of the world
I begin to contemplate
what I have done and left
undone, but this year
not so much rebuilding

of my perennially damaged
psyche, shoring up eroding
friendships, digging out
stumps of old resentments
that refuse to rot on their own.

No, this year I want to call
myself to task for what
I have done and not done
for peace. How much have
I dared in opposition?

How much have I put
on the line for freedom?
For mine and others?
As these freedoms are pared,
sliced and diced, where

have I spoken out? Who
have I tried to move? In
this holy season, I stand
self-convicted of sloth
in a time when lies choke

the mind and rhetoric
bends reason to slithering
choking pythons. Here
I stand before the gates
opening, the fire dazzling

my eyes, and as I approach
what judges me, I judge
myself. Give me weapons
of minute destruction. Let
my words turn into sparks.

Ne'ilah

The hinge of the year
the great gates opening
and then slowly slowly
closing on us.

I always imagine those gates
hanging over the ocean
fiery over the stone grey
waters of evening.

We cast what we must
change about ourselves
onto the waters flowing
to the sea. The sins,

errors, bad habits, whatever
you call them, dissolve.
When I was little I cried
out *I! I! I! I want, I want.*

Older, I feel less important,
a worker bee in the hive
of history, miles of hard
labor to make my sweetness.

The gates are closing
The light is failing

I kneel before what I love
imploring that it may live.

So much breaks, wears
down, fails in us. We must
forgive our broken promises—
their sharp shards in our hands.

A horizon of ghosts

You know how often I think of you
ranged there on the far shore
of nothing—with my dead friends,
my cats, all of you in a row watching.

Woody used to say he imagined
his father in the afterlife playing
cards. When Woody spoke his name
at Yischor on Yom Kippur,

Marvin would be called from the room
and be glad to be remembered.
Returning to his buddies, he'd
say, *That was my son calling.*

Mother I can't imagine an after
life, but still in dreams you march
into my mind's room as you used to,
clutching clippings to share,

demanding attention like a drug
to which you had been addicted
years ago, but even the wish
was dry as those clippings.

So remembering is an act
of prayer, a time when you
wake from ashes and air
turning your face toward light.

In the sukkah

Open to the sky
as our lives truly are
for down upon us can rain
all that our world has to offer—
sun and sleet, bombs and debris,

bits of space junk, meteorites
the red and yellow leaves
just beginning to color
and drift like open wings
of butterflies spiraling down—

we sit in our makeshift hut
willfully transitory, dressed
with the fruit of harvest
pumpkins, apples and nuts.
This is the feast where we

are commanded to be glad,
to rejoice in the bounty of earth
fat or meager. We're exposed.
Seldom do we sit or sleep
outside in this cooling time

as the earth plunges
toward darkness and ice.
We hear owls, the surviving
crickets, the rustling of fast
small life in the underbrush,

the padding of raccoons,
coyotes howling at the full moon
from down in the marsh.
It is a kind of nakedness
to strip off our houses

like snails left unprotected
and let the stars poke
into our skulls till we seem
to fall upward. How intimate
we are now with the night.

Season of skinny candles

A row of tall skinny candles
burns quickly into the night
air, the shames* raised
over the rest
for its hard work.

Darkness rushes in
after the sun sinks
like a bright plug pulled.
Our eyes drown in night
thick as ink pudding.

When even the moon
starves to a sliver
of quicksilver
the little candles poke
holes in the blackness.

A time to eat fat
and oil, a time to gamble
for pennies and gambol

*shames: the middle candle that lights the others every night

around the table, a light
and easy holiday.

No disasters, no
repentance, just remember
and enjoy. The miracle
is really eight days
and nights without trouble.

The full moon of Nisan

The full moon of Nisan pulls us
almost every Jew under the sky
to a table. Like a tide composed
of tiny rivulets we head
purposefully toward our seders
laden with the flat tasteless
bread of haste.

The moon when it rises looks
like strawberry ice cream.
Then it pales to waxy cheese.
Then it soars pale and pitted
like matzoh, the old kind
round instead of square
dry and winking.

Nisan brings the matzoh moon
urging buds to open, urging
minds to fling their gates
wide on the night we become
slaves and then march out
to freedom past lintels
smeared with blood.

The seder's order

The songs we join in
are beeswax candles
burning with no smoke
a clean fire licking at the evening

our voices small flames quivering.
The songs string us like beads
on the hour. The ritual is
its own melody that leads us

where we have gone before
and hope to go again, the comfort
of year after year. Order:
we must touch each base

of the haggadah as we pass,
blessing, handwashing,
dipping this and that. Voices
half harmonize on the *brukhahs*.

Dear faces like a multitude
of moons hang over the table
and the truest brief blessing:
affection and peace that we make.

Peace in a time of war

A puddle of amber light
like sun spread on a table,
food flirting savor into the nose,
faces of friends, a vase
of daffodils and Dutch iris:

this is an evening of honey
on the tongue, cinnamon
scented, red wine sweet
and dry, voices rising
like a flock of swallows

turning together in evening
air. Darkness walls off
the room from what lies
outside, the fire and dust
and blood of war, bodies

stacked like firewood
burst like overripe melons.
Ceremony is a moat we have
crossed into a moment's
harmony, as if the world paused—

but it doesn't. What we must
do waits like coats tossed
on the bed, for us to rise
from this warm table,
put on again and go out.

The cup of Eliyahu

In life you had a temper.
Your sarcasm was a whetted knife.
Sometimes you shuddered with fear
but you made yourself act no matter
how few stood with you.
Open the door for Eliyahu
that he may come in.

Now you return to us
in rough times, out of smoke
and dust that swirls blinding us.
You come in vision, you come
in lightning on blackness.
Open the door for Eliyahu
that he may come in.

In every generation you return
speaking what few want to hear
words that burn us, that cut
us loose so we rise and go again
over the sharp rocks upward.
Open the door for Eliyahu
that he may come in.

You come as a wild man,
as a homeless sidewalk orator,
you come as a woman taking the bima,

you come in prayer and song,
you come in a fierce rant.
Open the door for Eliyahu
that she may come in.

Prophecy is not a gift, but
sometimes a curse, Jonah
refusing. It is dangerous
to be right, to be righteous.
To stand against the wall of might.
Open the door for Eliyahu
that he may come in.

There are moments for each
of us when you summon, when
you call the whirlwind, when you
shake us like a rattle: then we
too must become you and rise.
Open the door for Eliyahu
that we may come in.

ACKNOWLEDGMENTS

"A vision of horses and mules," *Ploughshares*, Spring 2005, Vol. 31, No. 1.

"Sur l'ile Saint Louis," Wm. Meredith festschrift.

"Muttering," *Earth's Daughters*, No. 64, 2003.

"The Crooked Inheritance," *Earth's Daughters*, Spring 2006.

"Swear it," *Urban Spaghetti*, No. 5, 2004.

"The streets of Detroit were lined with elms," *The Southern California Anthology*, Vol. XVI, Fall 1999.

"Seven horses," *The Southern California Anthology*, Vol. XIV, 1997.

"Dress up," *Silver Visions II, Visions International #72*, 25th anniversary edition, 2005.

"I met a woman who wasn't there," *NWSA Journal*, 2006.

"Local street flooding is expected," *New York City Law Review*, 2006.

"Pick a number," "The closet of doom," "The Hollywood haircut," *Red Rock Review*, 2006.

"Dislocation," *Pebble Lake Review*, Vol. II, No. 1, Fall 2004.

"The special one," *Runes*, Winter Solstice 2003.

"My grandmother's song," *Lilith*, Summer 2003.

"The orphan," *Connecticut Review*, Vol. XXVI, No. 1, Spring 2004.

"The stray," *Many Mountains Moving*, Vol. 6, No. 2, October 2004.

"In St. Mawes," *Square Lake*, No. 5, Spring 2004.

"Famous lovers stumbled upon," *New Letters*, Vol. 71, No. 4, 2005.

"A long and busy night," "Mighty big," *Tapestries,* October 2005.
"In praise of java," *Tapestries,* No. 3, 2003.

"Peace in a time of war," *Tikkun,* Vol. 19, No. 5, September/October 2004.
"The birthday of the world," *Tikkun,* Vol. 18, No. 3, September/October 2003.

"Ne'ilah," *Midstream,* Vol. L, No. 6, September/October 2004.
"The order of the seder," *Midstream,* Vol. L, No. 3, April 2004.
"The late year," *Midstream,* September/October 2002.
"The cup of Eliyahu," *Midstream,* Vol. XXXXIX, No. 3, April 2003.

"The moon as cat as peach," *Lunar Calendar,* Luna Press, 1997.
"The month of aspirin," *Lunar Calendar,* Luna Press, 2005.

"Fagged out," *Caprice,* January 1999.
"Portrait of the poet as a young nerd," *Caprice,* Vol. XIX: 1, Spring 2004.

"The dawn of nothing," *Verve,* Vol. 9, No. 1, Spring 1997.

"Choose a color," *Stinging Fly* (Irish publication), Issue 1, Vol. 2, Spring 2005.
"Choose a color," *The Seattle Review,* Vol. XXVII, No. 2, 2005.
"Buried," *The Seattle Review,* Vol. XXVII, No. 2, 2005.

"Rotten," "Tanks in the streets," *Blue Collar Review,* Vol. 8, Issue 2, Winter
    2004–2005.
"Motown, Arsenal of Democracy," *Blue Collar Review,* Vol. 7, Issue 4, Summer 2004.

"National monument: Castle Clinton," "Minor characters," *Prairie Schooner,*
    Summer 2005.

"Absolutely safe," *Kalliope,* Vol. XXVI, No. 1, 2004.
"Intense," "At the core of loving, fear," *Kalliope,* Vol. XXV, No. 2, 2003.
"Hurricane warning," "White night," *Kalliope,* Vol. XXVII, No. 2, 2005.

"Money is one of those things," *Chiron Review,* Issue 71, Summer 2003.
"Deadlocked wedlock," *Stinging Fly* (Irish publication), Issue 1, Vol. 2, Spring 2005;
    Chiron Review, Issue 79, Summer 2005.

"Less than you bargained for," MR Webzine, July 15, 2005.

"Choices," *Monthly Review,* April 2003; *Irish Socialist Worker,* March 19, 2005.
"Sneak and peek," *Monthly Review,* Vol. 55, No. 7, 2003.

"In our name," *Monthly Review*, Vol. 56, No. 4, September 2004; *Irish Socialist Worker*, March 19, 2005.

"The young and the stupid," *Caprice*, August 1998.

"Bashert," *Caprice*, xix:2, Summer 2005.

"A horizon of ghosts," "The house is empty," *Blue Fifth Online*, Vol. V, Issue 3, July 2005.

"In the raw," *Blue Fifth Online*, Vol. II, Issue 2, March 2002.

"The lived in look," "Hot heart," *The Cape Cod Voice*, Literary Issue, Winter 2005.

"August like lint in the lungs," "Mated," *Paterson Literary Review*, Issue 34, 2005.

"How to make pesto," "More than enough," "Tracks," *Paterson Literary Review*, Issue 32, 2003.

A NOTE ABOUT THE AUTHOR

The Crooked Inheritance is Marge Piercy's seventeenth collection of poetry. Others include *Colors Passing Through Us; The Art of Blessing the Day; Early Grrrl; What are Big Girls Made Of?; Mars and Her Children; The Moon Is Always Female;* her selected poems *Circles on the Water; Stone, Paper, Knife;* and *My Mother's Body.* In 1990 her poetry won the Golden Rose, the oldest poetry award in the country. She is also the author of a memoir, *Sleeping with Cats,* and seventeen novels, the most recent being *Sex Wars.* Her fiction and poetry have been translated into sixteen languages. She lives on Cape Cod, with her husband, Ira Wood, the novelist and publisher of LeapFrog Press, with whom she has written a play, a novel, and most recently the second edition of *So You Want To Write: How to Master the Craft of Fiction and Personal Narrative.* Marge Piercy's Web site address is www.margepiercy.com.

A NOTE ON THE TYPE

This book was set in Monotype Dante, a typeface designed by Giovanni Mardersteig (1892–1977). Conceived as a private type for the Officina Bodoni in Verona, Italy, Dante was originally cut only for hand composition by Charles Malin, the famous Parisian punch cutter, between 1946 and 1952. Its first use was in an edition of Boccaccio's *Trattatello in laude di Dante* that appeared in 1954. The Monotype Corporation's version of Dante followed in 1957. Although modeled on the Aldine type used for Pietro Cardinal Bembo's treatise *De Aetna* in 1495, Dante is a thoroughly modern interpretation of the venerable face.

Composed by Stratford Publishing Services, Brattleboro, Vermont

Printed and bound by R. R. Donnelley, Harrisonburg, Virginia

Designed by Robert C. Olsson